Witches

Aaron Frisch

CREATIVE ◖ EDUCATION

Published by
Creative Education
P.O. Box 227
Mankato, Minnesota 56002
Creative Education
is an imprint of
The Creative Company
www.thecreativecompany.us

Design and production by
Christine Vanderbeek
Art direction by **Rita Marshall**
Printed in the United States of America

Photographs by Alamy (AF Archive, Pictorial Press Ltd), Dreamstime (Tomasz Boinski, Fernando Gregory, Sarah Holmlund, Marina Pissarova), Getty Images (Joshua Ets-Hokin, Oleksiy Maksymenko, David Young-Wolff), iStockphoto (Michael Courtney, Sean Locke, Leo Kowal), Mary Evans Picture Library (WARNER BROS AND J K ROWLING / Ronald Grant Archive), Shutterstock (Anneka, Mikhail, Tupungato, Kiselev Andrey Valerevich)

Library of Congress
Cataloging-in-Publication Data
Frisch, Aaron.
Witches / Aaron Frisch.
p. cm. — (That's spooky!)
Summary: A basic but fun exploration of witches—women with magical or supernatural powers—including how they come to exist, their weaknesses, and memorable examples from pop culture. Includes bibliographical references and index.
ISBN 978-1-60818-250-3
1. Witches—Juvenile literature. 2. Women—Miscellanea—Juvenile literature. I. Title.

BF1571.5.W66F75 2013
133.4'3—dc23 2011051182

First edition
9 8 7 6 5 4 3 2 1

CONTENTS

IMAGINE ...

You are walking along a country road at **TWILIGHT**. You hear a cackling laugh. Then you feel a whoosh of air. Suddenly, you see a woman in a pointy black hat riding a broom across the sky!

IT'S A WITCH!

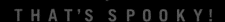

THAT'S SPOOKY!

WHAT IS A WITCH?

A witch is a woman who can do magic. A witch's magic is called witchcraft. Only women can be witches. A man who has powers like a witch is called a warlock or a wizard.

Most witches and warlocks dress in black

BECOMING A WITCH

Some people are born witches. They grow up with magical powers. Other women become witches by learning to do magic. There are good witches and bad witches. Bad witches use magic for evil.

Learning witchcraft can take a lot of practice

WITCH BEHAVIOR

Bad witches might use magic to get **REVENGE** or to do other mean things. Witches do most of their work at night. They read books of **SPELLS**. Many witches keep black cats as pets.

Most witches keep thick books of spells handy

A WITCH'S POWERS

A witch might use a **CAULDRON**. She puts special things into the cauldron and boils them like a soup. This helps her make **POTIONS**. Some witches can fly by riding a broom, too.

A witch's cauldron might be as big as a bathtub

A WITCH'S WEAKNESSES

It can be hard to stop a witch's magic after she has cast a spell. People might burn evil witches to kill them. In some movies, witches melt if they get water on them!

Even most witchcraft cannot stop a fire

FAMOUS WITCHES

Most witches in stories and movies are bad. One of the most famous witches is the Wicked Witch of the West from the story *The Wizard of Oz*. She does evil magic and controls flying monkeys!

The Wicked Witch of the West and a flying monkey

16

In the fairy tale "Snow White," a witch gives Snow White a poisoned apple that makes her fall asleep for a long time. The *Harry Potter* books and movies are about kids who go to a special school to learn witchcraft.

Snow White (left); Harry Potter doing magic (above)

CRUISE ON A BROOM

Witches who can do magic are not real. They exist only in stories. But acting like a witch can be fun. Get a pointy witch hat and a broom, and then "fly" around your house or yard. This works best at night!

A witch's broom can be a fun way to get around

pointy hat

warty nose

black cloak

greenish skin

THAT'S SPOOKY!

LEARN TO SPOT A WITCH

DICTIONARY

CAULDRON a big pot used to boil things over a fire

POTIONS drinks or liquids that are poisonous or have magical powers

REVENGE do something bad to people because they did something bad to you

SPELLS special sayings that make magic happen

TWILIGHT the time of day when the sun sets and the sky gets dark

THAT'S SPOOKY!
WITCHES

READ MORE

Besel, Jennifer M. *Witches*. Mankato, Minn.: Capstone, 2007.

Leuck, Laura. *One Witch*. New York: Walker, 2003.

Marzollo, Jean. *I Spy Spooky Night: A Book of Picture Riddles*. New York: Scholastic, 1996.

WEB SITES

FUNSCHOOL: HALLOWEEN

http://funschool.kaboose.com/fun-blaster/halloween/

This site has a lot of spooky games and pictures for coloring.

THE KIDZ PAGE: HALLOWEEN WITCH GAME

http://www.thekidzpage.com/halloween_games/free-kids-halloween-games/halloween-game1.html

Help a witch fly through the night sky in this video game.

INDEX